101 Reasons Why Cats Make Great Kids

Allia Zobel

Illustrations by Nicole Hollander

ADAMS MEDIA CORPORATION
Holbrook, Massachusetts

Published by Adams Media Corporation
260 Center Street, Holbrook, MA 02343

ISBN: 1-55850-639-X

Printed in Korea.

J I H G F E D C B A

This book is available at quantity discounts for bulk purchases.
For information, call 1-800-872-5627
(in Massachusetts, call 617-767-8100).

Visit our home page at http://www.adamsmedia.com

For God; my husband, Desmond Finbarr Nolan; my sister, Vicky, and her twelve natural-born kids (my favorite nieces and nephews): Frankie, Joseph, Judy, Alex, Catalina, Maria, Tuki, Max, Mercy, Magdalena, Margarita, and Emily, who, though they are not cats, are the next best thing.

— A.Z.

This book is for all those men and women who gave birth to furry children, and, of course, to my progeny, Izzy, Eric, and Buddy.

— N.H.

For Brandon Toropov, my agent, and the gang at Adams Media Corporation.

— A.Z.

Introduction

CHILDREN ARE LIFE'S MOST PRECIOUS GIFT. That's a given. But for some of us, they are not a reality. So must we forgo the joys of parenthood? Never hear the pitter-patter of little feet? Never see that gaze of unconditional love?

NOT! While I will never be a parent in the true sense of the word, I am a mama nevertheless, with two adorable offspring, Vanessa and Winston-Stanley, III, to prove it. And although there is little resemblance (except, some say, around the whiskers), they are as much my babies as if I had had the litter myself. What's more, when I look into their yellow-green eyes, I know, without as much as a faint meow, that they love me just as much and believe I'm their mama too.

Indeed, I am not a lone crackpot (although some may dispute this). Truth is, I can point to lots of folks who share their hearts and homes with sons and daughters who swat spiders and walk on four legs instead of two. And, like myself, I've never heard them wish it were any other way.

So, as far as I'm concerned, I have the perfect alternative family. Okay, so Winston-Stanley will never grow up to become a famous doctor. And Vanessa won't marry a wealthy lawyer and have a dozen kids who look just like their "Gran." On the other hand, with my looks and genes, any "real" kid of mine probably wouldn't either.

I guess what I'm trying to say is that our progeny are there to love and be loved, no matter what form they take. Mine just happen to be beautiful, intelligent, warm, playful, and dependable, with wet noses that can smell a can of tuna a mile away.

Of course, when we get right down to it, none of us, no matter who we are and how we boast, can ever really have perfect children. But I'd have to say that my babies, Vanessa and Winston-Stanley, come *awfully* close. Enjoy!

— A.Z.

You never have to change a diaper—
and toilet-training is a snap.

Cats love it when you call them your "baby."

You don't have to teach cats about the "birds and the bees."

Cats are eager to follow in your footsteps.

I Believe that Piercing violates the essential integrity of the Body.

Mr. Large

A CAT WILL NEVER BEG YOU TO LET HIM HAVE HIS NOSE PIERCED.

NO ONE WILL ARREST YOU IF YOU LEAVE YOUR CAT UNSUPERVISED FOR AN EVENING.

An allowance is optional.

You don't have to worry if your cat stays out all night (though you probably will).

Cats always look up to you.

Cats eat it up when you brag about them.

No matter what your car looks like,
cats love to go for a ride.

Cats don't mind if they have an overbite.
What's more, you'll never go in hock for braces.

A cat would never leave you for his biological mother.

Cats don't need help with their homework.

CATS APPRECIATE WHEN YOU KNIT FOR THEM.

CATS ADORE WEARING MOTHER-AND DAUGHTER LOOK-ALIKE OUTFITS.

Cats don't eat junk food and spoil their dinners.

You will never have to sit through your cat's rendition of "Annie."

Cats never bring home bad report cards.

Cats love to go to the office with Daddy.

CATS COULDN'T GIVE A HOOT ABOUT BARNEY. THEY'D MUCH PREFER TO PLAY WITH THEIR "MOMMY," — YOU.

YOU CAN TAKE AS MANY PHOTOS OF YOUR
CAT AS YOU LIKE AND SHE'LL NEVER COMPLAIN.

You never have to buy cats expensive toys, unless, of course, you want to.

You never have to harp on your cat to wash up. And she never misses behind her ears.

Cats are too couth to have burping contests.

Cats adore outward displays of affection.

Cats are never too busy with their own lives to sit and chat.

Cats can't pick up your bad habits.

Cats never grow up.

Cats look forward to going to "Grandma's" for the weekend.

WOULDN'T it be FUN to HAVE A KITTEN AROUND?

JUST TRY it!

ANOTHER CAT MIGHT DAMAGE the EMOTIONAL BALANCE WE'VE WORKED SO HARD to ACHIEVE.

CATS THINK BEING AN ONLY CHILD IS NEAT.

Cats never wreck the house when you're away.
(They do it while you're there.)

Though he may ignore you, a cat
will never sass you.

You never have to worry about your cat's teenage hormones.

Cats don't pick their noses.

CATS MAKE A BIG DEAL OUT OF MOTHER'S DAY.

CATS DON'T MIND IF YOU PLAY FAVORITES...
AS LONG AS THEY'RE THE FAVORITE.

Your cat won't insist you put her drawings on the refrigerator. (But if you don't, she'll probably pout for a week.)

Cats enjoy going on trips with their parents. What's more, they never say, "Are we there yet?"

You never have to write your cat's teacher an absentee note.

Cats love liver and eat all their greens.

CATS LOVE to CRAWL IN BED WITH YOU.

It's not necessary to keep up with your cat's friends' parents.

Cats don't need chauffeuring to and from soccer, cheerleading, or band practice.

Cats couldn't care less about MTV.

You never have to teach your cat to ride a bike or drive a car.

CATS ARE A BLESSING IN YOUR OLD AGE.

Cats don't ask you to wire money—
unless it's a dire emergency.

You don't have to buy expensive
designer clothes for a cat.
A simple ruby or sapphire collar will suffice.

Though he may hang out and sing with his friends, a cat would never start a rap group and practice in your cellar.

You never have to argue with your cat about taking a nap.

CATS HAVE 20/20 VISION. SO YOU SAVE ON EYEGLASSES AND CONTACTS.

You never have to chase the bogeyman from under the bed; your cat will do it for you.

Cats are thrilled to spend holidays with their aunts and uncles.

Cats don't have noisy sleepovers;
theirs are quiet and civilized.

Cats don't hog the computer.
Two or three hours a day on the
Internet and they're more than satisfied.

You can trust a cat with the family secrets.

Cats can't wait to go hunting with Dad.

Cats keep their rooms clean.

Cats love you just the way you are.

Cats let you know when you're out of milk.

A CAT IS NOT EMBARRASSED TO KISS HIS MOM IN FRONT OF HIS FRIENDS.

CATS ARE ALWAYS VERY COMPLIMENTARY,
NO MATTER WHAT YOU WEAR.

It doesn't bother a cat if you're
a single mom or dad.

Cats enjoy helping you make the beds.

You don't have to throw expensive bar mitzvah or sweet sixteen parties—unless, of course, your cat insists.

You never have to be afraid your cat will spike his hair and dye it purple.

CATS LOVE BEING PART
OF THE FAMILY.

Cats don't need dates for the Junior Prom.

Cats don't borrow your makeup—
except in emergencies.

Cats don't make comparisons.
When it comes to dads, you're tops.

A cat would never, like, use, like,
the word "like" all the time.

CATS NEVER GET BORED LISTENING TO STORIES ABOUT WHEN YOU WERE YOUNG.

Cats don't care how much money you make.

Cats don't talk about you in therapy.

Cats are big on togetherness.

You can sleep through your cat's twelve o'clock feeding.

CATS ALWAYS LOOK UP TO YOU.

A cat would never elope and deprive you of a wedding.

You'll save a bundle on mountain bikes and in-line skates. Cats prefer playing with grocery bags and rubber bands.

You never have to worry about your cat's self-esteem.

A cat would never ask you for a nose job for her birthday.

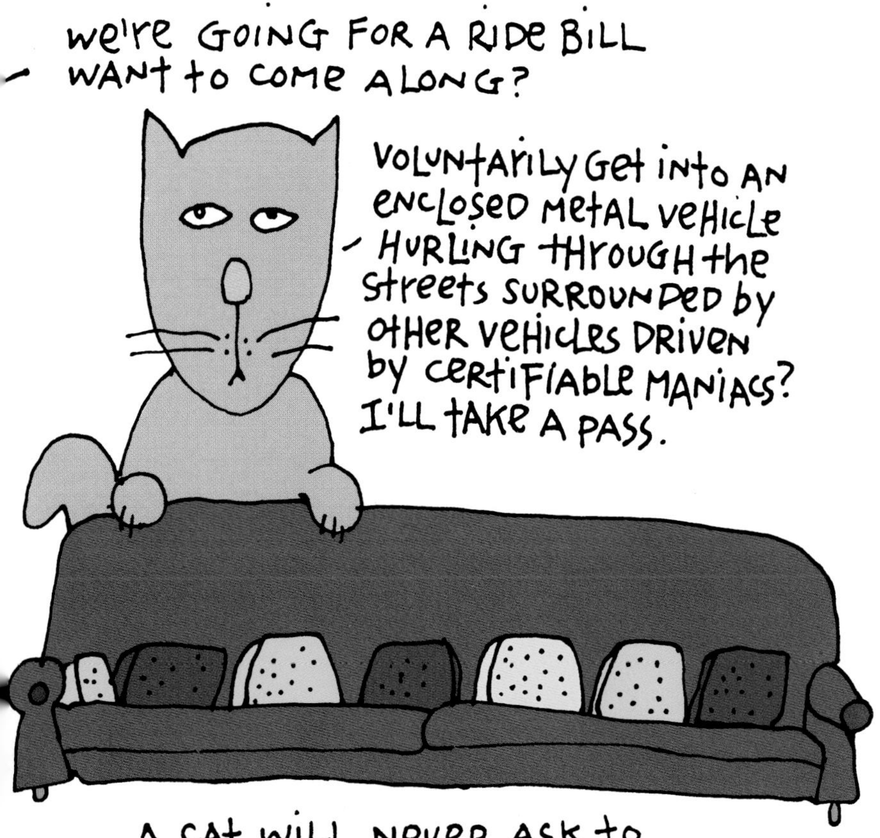

A CAT WILL NEVER ASK TO BORROW YOUR CAR KEYS.

CATS DON'T MIND HELPING WITH THE DISHES.

A cat's imaginary friend is you.

You never have to pace the waiting room
while your cat has his tonsils out.

Cats don't expect you to watch Sesame Street with them.

A cat won't walk around all day plugged into a portable CD player.

CATS TAKE AN interest in your Hobbies. they love FISHING WITH DAD AND BiRD WATCHING WITH MOM.

Cats will share their Halloween treats.

Cats always listen when you tell them something for their own good.

Cats are proud to have you as their Mom.

About the Author

Allia Zobel is also the author of *Women Who Love Cats Too Much*, *101 Reasons Why a Cat Is Better than a Man*, *The Joy of Being Single*, and *Younger Men Are Better than Retin-A*. She lives in Bridgeport, Connecticut.

About the Illustrator

Nicole Hollander's nationally syndicated comic strip *Sylvia* has a devoted following from coast to coast. She is also the illustrator of *Women Who Love Cats Too Much* and *101 Reasons Why a Cat Is Better than a Man*. Ms. Hollander lives in Chicago, Illinois.